Memento

A selection of award-winning photography
from Getty Images

Una selección de fotografías premiadas,
presentadas por Getty Images

La sélection de photos primées de
Getty Images

Eine Auswahl preisgekrönter Fotografien
von Getty Images

The award-winning photograph surprises us about our world

Foreword by Cornell Capa
Founding Director Emeritus
International Center of Photography
New York

This book is a collage of everyday life.

It's the hard news images we see in our newspaper in the morning; the advertising images in the magazines we flick through in the office; the sports images we graze looking for the results of our favorite team.

No matter what the content, all the award-winning images here do one thing. It does not matter whether it is shot by a news photographer working alone on the front line, or whether taken by a photographer working with models, stylists, an Art Director and a gaggle of 150 extras.

The award-winning photograph surprises us about our world.

Spoiled by professional excellence, we expect quality, skill and simple good value. The great image gives us the gift of surprise. In our image-rich world the great photograph takes us out of our professional space and brings us to somewhere we could not have imagined, shows us something we have not seen. The truly inspiring image delivers an emotion or idea beyond its brief.

The award-winning photo goes beyond the conditions necessary for its creation. We all know what it takes to deliver.

It is the news photographer who has a nose for a story and the bloody-minded willfulness to chase down the image that nails it.

It is the sports photographer who knows the best location at an event, knows where to direct the camera to get that image of competitive desire, athletic poetry or sheer ecstasy.

Or the advertising photographer whose art director has been briefed on the visual trends that will definitively capture the zeitgeist.

But these are just parts of the collage, things that just might, on a good day, offer the possibility of greatness. Greatness is when everything clicks; the research, the light, the event, the subjects, the model, the camera, the photographer. Everything converges on that one moment when the image clicks with the viewer in an unexpected way.

French writer Roland Barthes called this the 'punctum' of the photograph. He said it is that one thing in the image that is beyond calculation, 'that accident which pricks me (but also bruises me, is poignant to me).'

All the images in this book deliver that accident born from professionalism.

En él encontramos las imágenes de candente actualidad que vemos en el periódico de la mañana; las imágenes publicitarias de las revistas que hojeamos en la oficina; las imágenes deportivas que apenas registramos al buscar los resultados del último partido de nuestro equipo favorito.

Independientemente de su contenido, todas estas imágenes premiadas tienen algo en común. Tanto da que el autor sea un reportero gráfico trabajando solo en el centro de noticia, o un fotógrafo trabajando con modelos, estilistas, director artístico y un ejército de 150 figurantes.

La mejor fotografía nos sorprende con su forma de ver el mundo.

Acostumbrados a la excelencia profesional, hoy ponemos el listón muy alto, exigiendo calidad, talento y buen precio. Una gran imagen nos ofrece el valioso regalo de la sorpresa. En un mundo colmado de imágenes, una gran fotografía nos saca de nuestro medio profesional para llevarnos a espacios que no hubiésemos podido imaginar, nos muestra algo que nunca hemos visto. La imagen verdaderamente capaz de inspirar comunica una emoción o una idea que trasciende los requisitos del encargo.

La mejor fotografía va más allá de las condiciones necesarias para su creación. Y todos sabemos lo que se pone en juego para conseguirla.

sabe reconocer una historia y persigue con obstinación irrenunciable la imagen que la refleja.

La experiencia de un fotógrafo deportivo que sabe cuál es la mejor ubicación en un evento y sabe hacia dónde dirigir la cámara para captar esa imagen de espíritu competitivo al desnudo, de poesía atlética o puro éxtasis.

O la garra de un fotógrafo publicitario cuyo director artístico ha recabado toda la información sobre las tendencias visuales que capturarán el espíritu de la época.

Pero todos estos elementos sólo son parte del collage; variables que podrían, en un momento dado, ofrecer una oportunidad de alcanzar la grandeza. La grandeza sólo se consigue cuando todo funciona: la investigación, la luz, la oportunidad, los temas, el modelo, la cámara... el fotógrafo. Todo converge en ese momento singular en que la imagen conecta con el espectador de forma inesperada.

El escritor francés Roland Barthes llamó el "punctum" de la fotografía a ese elemento de la imagen que no se puede prever, "ese accidente que me punza pero también me lastima, me inquieta)".

Todas las imágenes de este libro contienen ese "accidente" nacido de la profesionalidad.

Une photo primée provoque une émotion inattendue.

Avant-propos de Cornell Capa
Founding Director Emeritus
International Center of Photography
New York

Ce livre est un collage de notre vie.

Il nous montre des images violentes d'actualité que nous voyons tous les matins dans nos journaux ; les photos publicitaires des magazines que nous feuilletons au bureau ; les photos de sport que nous dévorons en attendant les résultats de notre équipe favorite.

Q'importe leur contenu, toutes ces photos provoquent le même effet, qu'elles aient été prises par un reporter travaillant seul en première ligne ou un photographe entouré de mannequins, de stylistes, d'un directeur artistique et de cent cinquante figurants, toutes les images primées regroupées ici produisent le même effet.

Une photo primée provoque une émotion inattendue.

Convaincus de la maîtrise technique, nous attendons désormais de la qualité, de la compétence et de la satisfaction. Une bonne photo nous offre un cadeau : l'étonnement. Dans notre monde riche en images, le grand photographe est celui qui nous sort de notre univers professionnel, nous emmène là où nous n'imaginions pas et nous montre ce que nous n'avions pas vu. La photo vraiment envoûtante génère une émotion ou une idée qui va au-delà de son dessein premier.

Une photo primée dépasse les conditions nécessaires à sa création et nous savons tous très bien ce que cela exige.

C'est le reporter qui flaire le bon sujet et affiche une volonté farouche de prendre la photo.

C'est le photographe de sport qui sait où se placer lors d'un événement et où diriger son appareil pour obtenir la photo qui illustre la volonté de vaincre, la force ou le plaisir. C'est le photographe publicitaire briefé par son directeur artistique sur les tendances visuelles qui réussit à immortaliser l'air du temps.

Mais il ne s'agit là que de simples morceaux du collage, de choses qui peuvent, quand la chance est là, révéler leur grandeur. La grandeur, c'est quand tout fait tilt : la recherche, la lumière, l'événement, les sujets, le mannequin, l'appareil photo et le photographe. Tout converge vers ce moment où l'image fait tilt de façon inattendue sur celui qui la regarde.

C'est ce que l'écrivain Roland Barthes a baptisé le "punctum" de la photographie. Il affirmait que c'était le détail particulier q ui est au-dessus de tout calcul : "ce hasard qui, dans une photo à la fois me 'point', mais aussi me meurtrit."

Dans toutes les photos de ce livre, on retrouve ce hasard né du professionnalisme.

Preisgekrönte Fotografien enthüllen Überraschendes über unsere Welt

Vorwort von Cornell Capa
Founding Director Emeritus
International Center of Photography
New York

Eine Collage des täglichen Lebens.

Dieses Buch zeigt uns die Bilder zu den Schlagzeilen, die wir jeden Morgen in der Zeitung lesen, die Werbeaufnahmen aus den Magazinen, durch die wir im Büro blättern, und die Sportfotos, die uns auf der Suche nach den Ergebnissen unserer Lieblingsteams ins Auge stechen.

Ganz gleich, ob die Fotos von einem einzelnen Nachrichtenfotografen am Kriegsschauplatz oder von einem Modefotografen mit seiner Entourage aus Models, Stylisten, einem Art Director und 150 Komparsen aufgenommen wurden: Unabhängig von ihrem Inhalt haben diese preisgekrönten Bilder alle eines gemeinsam.

Preisgekrönte Fotografien enthüllen Überraschendes über unsere Welt.

Wir, die wir herausragende professionelle Leistungen gewöhnt sind, erwarten stets Qualität, berufliches Können und einfach gute Bilder. Ein großartiges Bild aber hält immer Überraschungen bereit. Es transportiert Emotionen und Ideen, die über den eigentlichen Fotoauftrag hinausgehen. In unserer mit Bildern überladenen Welt sind es eben diese großartigen Fotografien, die uns an einen Ort jenseits unserer Vorstellungskraft bringen und uns etwas zeigen, das wir so noch nie gesehen haben.

Ein preisgekröntes Foto übertrifft die bloßen Voraussetzungen der Aufnahme. Wir alle wissen, was es heißt, solche Bilder zu schießen.

Der Nachrichtenfotograf, mit dem richtigen Riecher für die Story, der stur bis zum Schmerz sein muss und die Bilder einfängt, die so noch niemand gesehen hat.

Der Sportfotograf, der für seine Fotos stundenlang am Spielfeldrand kauert, der weiß, wohin er die Kamera richten muss, um den Kampfgeist, die athletische Poesie und die schiere Ekstase im Bild einzufangen.

Oder der Werbefotograf, der mit seinem Art Director Trends und Strömungen einfängt, die den Zeitgeist bis ins kleinste Detail widerspiegeln.

All das sind nur Teile der Collage. Dinge, die einer Fotografie eventuell Größe verleihen. Größe entsteht, wenn alles zusammenpasst: Creative Research, das Licht, der Ort, die Themen, das Model, die Kamera – der Fotograf. Wenn sich dies alles in dem kurzen Augenblick trifft, in dem sich der Verschluss öffnet, dann offenbart sich dem Betrachter ein großartiges Bild.

Der französische Schriftsteller Roland Barthes nennt dies das 'Punctum' der Fotografie. Es beschreibt das, was man nicht ausrechnen kann: „Das Zufällige, das mich besticht (mich aber auch verwundet, mich trifft)."

Die Bilder in diesem Buch besitzen Punctum.

It would be very interesting to preserve photographically not the stages but the metamorphoses of a picture. Possibly one might then discover the path followed by the brain in materialising a dream.
Pablo Picasso, Spanish painter and sculptor

Fotografía creativa

Sería muy curioso conservar fotográficamente no las etapas de un cuadro, sino su metamorfosis. Tal vez se percibiría la senda por donde el cerebro se dirige hacia la materialización de su sueño.
Pablo Picasso, pintor y escultor español

Photographie créative

Il serait très intéressant de conserver photographiquement non pas les étapes, mais les métamorphoses d'une image. Peut-être alors découvrirait-on le chemin suivi par le cerveau pour matérialiser un rêve.
Pablo Picasso, peintre et sculpteur espagnol

Kreative Fotografie

Es wäre sehr interessant, wenn man
nicht nur die einzelnen Phasen eines
Bildes fotografisch festhalten könnte,
sondern seine Metamorphose.
Möglicherweise könnte man dann
den Weg erkennen, dem das Gehirn bei
der Verwirklichung eines Traumes folgt.
Pablo Picasso, spanischer Maler
und Bildhauer

Tim Flach

Gold
Association of Photographers 2003

A picture can become for us a
highway between a particular thing
and a universal feeling.
Lauren Harris, English novelist

Un cuadro puede convertirse para
nosotros en el camino entre algo
particular y un sentimiento universal.
Lauren Harris, novelista inglesa

Une image peut devenir pour nous une
autoroute reliant une chose particulière
à un sentiment universel.
Lauren Harris, romancière anglaise

Ein Bild kann für uns zu einer Schnellstraße
werden zwischen einer bestimmten Sache
und einem universellen Gefühl.
Lauren Harris, englische Schriftstellerin

Photo District News Photo Annual 2003

Enter these enchanted woods, you
who dare.
George Meredith, British novelist and poet

Entrad en este bosque encantado,
quienes oséis hacerlo.
George Meredith, novelista y poeta inglés

Pénétrez ces bois enchantés,
vous qui osez.
George Meredith, romancier et poète anglais

So betretet nun diesen verzauberten Wald,
ihr Wagemutigen.
George Meredith, englischer Schriftsteller
und Dichter

Silver
Association of Photographers 2003

Photo District News Photo Annual 2002

Art Director: Paul Foster

There is no excellent beauty that hath
not some strangeness in the proportion.
Sir Francis Bacon, English philosopher
and statesman

No hay belleza sin algo extraño en
sus proporciones.
Sir Francis Bacon, filósofo y
estadista inglés

Il n'y a point de beauté exceptionnelle sans
quelque bizarrerie dans les proportions.
Sir Francis Bacon, homme d'Etat et
philosophe anglais

Es gibt keine herausragende Schönheit,
die nicht etwas Außergewöhnliches in ihren
Proportionen hat.
Sir Francis Bacon, englischer Staatsmann
und Philosoph

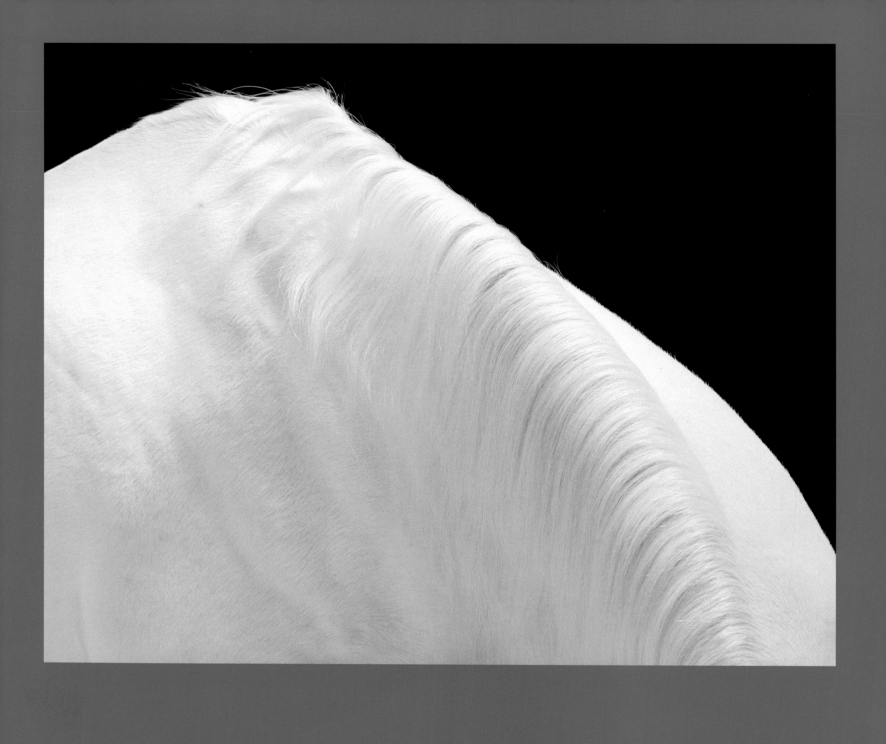

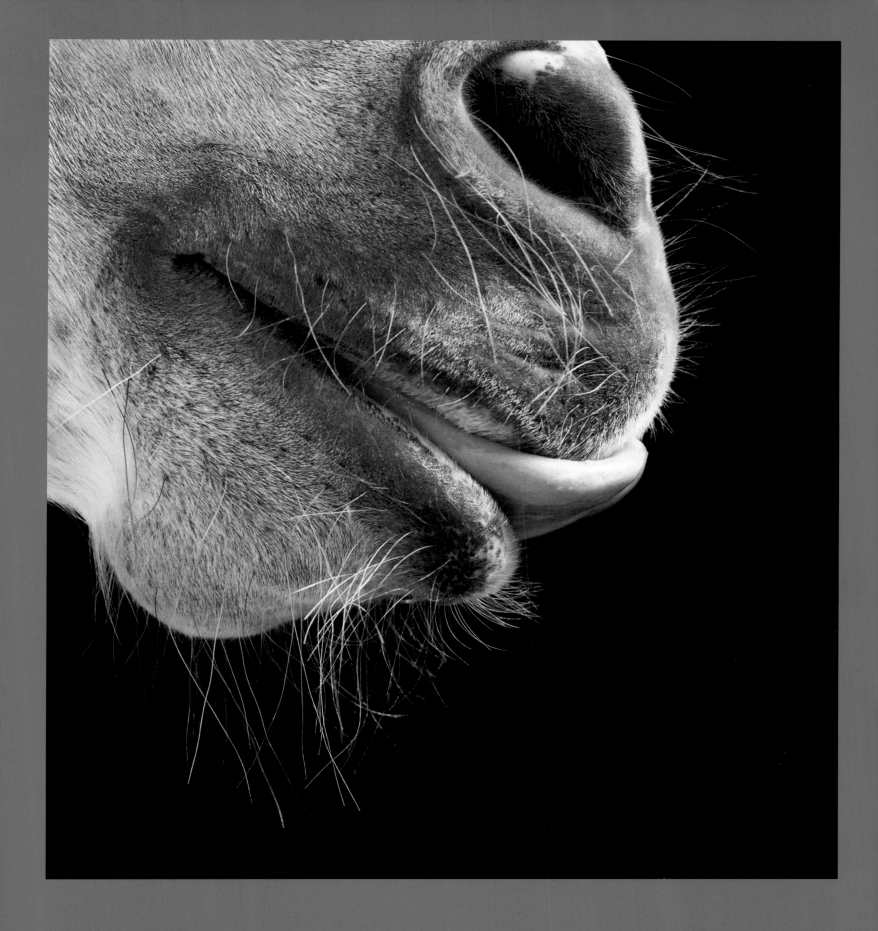

Tim MacPherson

Communication Arts Photography Annual
2002

Art Director: Rhiannon Llewellyn

A person needs a little madness, or else
they never dare cut the rope and be free.
Nikos Kazantzakis, Greek philosopher
and writer

Una persona necesita un poco de locura,
o nunca se atreverá a cortar las ligaduras
y ser libre.
Nikos Kazantzakis, filósofo y escritor griego

Toute personne doit avoir un soupçon
de folie, sinon elle n'osera jamais couper
la corde pour être libre.
Nikos Kazantzakis, philosophe et
écrivain grec

Man muss schon ein bisschen verrückt
sein, sonst würde man esnie wagen, seine
Fesseln zu zerschneiden, um frei zu sein.
Nikos Kazantzakis, griechischer Philosoph
und Schriftsteller

Communication Arts Photography Annual
2002

Art Director: Rhiannon Llewellyn

The whole of nature resides in every
model, and the eye capable of seeing
can discover it there.
Auguste Rodin, French sculptor

La naturaleza entera reside en cada
modelo, y allí puede descubrirla el ojo
capaz de ver.
Auguste Rodin, escultor francés

Il n'y a point de recette pour embellir
la nature. Il ne s'agit que de voir.
Auguste Rodin, sculpteur français

Die Ganzheit der Natur offenbart sich
in jedem Modell, und das Auge, das sieht,
kann sie dort erkennen.
Auguste Rodin, französischer Bildhauer

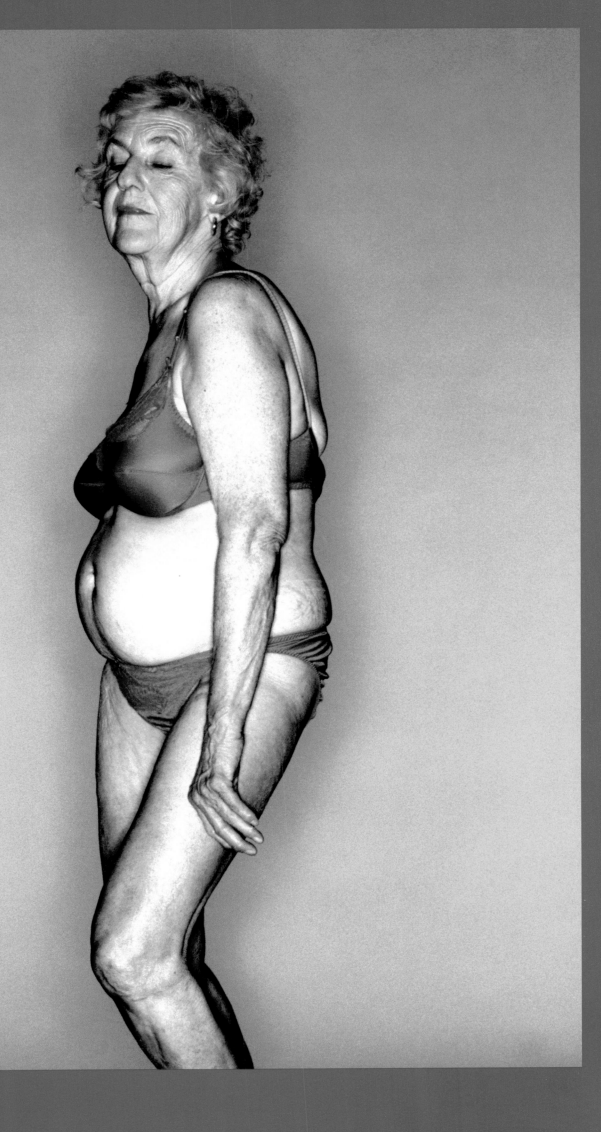

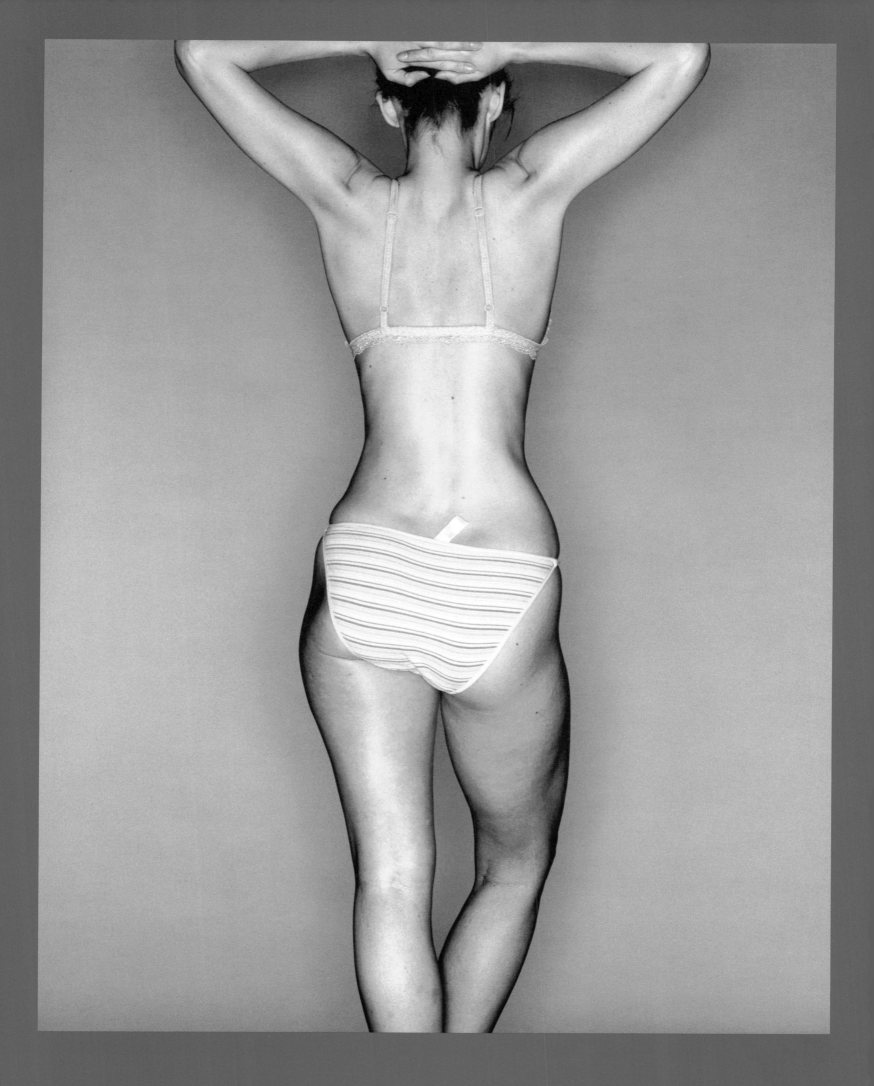

Association of Photographers 2002

Art Director: Rhiannon Llewellyn

A colour shines in its surroundings.
Just as eyes only smile in a face.
Ludwig Wittgenstein, Austrian philosopher

Un color sólo brilla en su entorno,
tal como los ojos sólo sonríen en un rostro.
Ludwig Wittgenstein, filósofo austríaco

Une couleur ne brille que dans son
environnement comme les yeux ne
sourient que dans un visage.
Ludwig Wittgenstein, philosophe autrichien

Eine Farbe wird erst durch ihre Umgebung
bedeutsam. So wie ein Gesicht nur mit
Augen lächeln kann.
Ludwig Wittgenstein, österreichischer
Philosoph

Kyoko Hamada

American Photography 18

Art Director: Jennifer Dorn

The longer you look at a thing the
more it transforms.
Anne Michaels, Canadian poet
and novelist

Cuanto más se mira algo, más ese
algo se transforma.
Anne Michaels, poeta y novelista
canadiense

Plus vous regardez une chose,
plus elle se transforme.
Anne Michaels, poète et romancière
canadienne

Je länger man etwas ansieht,
desto mehr verwandelt es sich.
Anne Michaels, kanadische Dichterin
und Schriftstellerin

Communication Arts Photography Annual
2001

Amercan Photography 18

Art Director: Lisa Thackaberry

The camera makes everyone a tourist
in other people's reality, and eventually
in one's own.
Susan Sontag, American writer and critic

La cámara convierte a cualquiera en turista
de la realidad de otras personas, y finalmente,
de la suya propia.
Susan Sontag, escritora y crítica
estadounidense

L'appareil photo fait de chacun un touriste
dans la réalité de l'autre, et finalement dans
sa propre réalité.
Susan Sontag, écrivain et critique américain

Die Kamera macht jeden zum Touristen
in der Realität des anderen und letztendlich
auch in der eigenen.
Susan Sontag, amerikanische Schriftstellerin
und Kritikerin

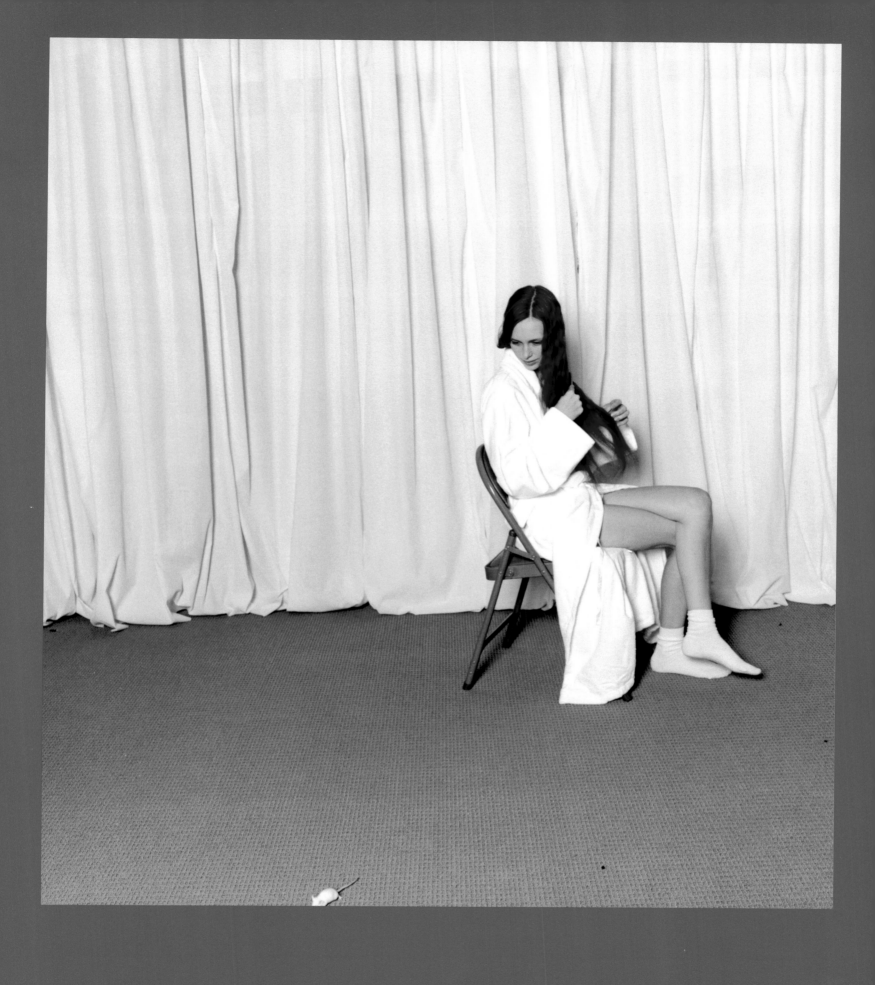

Shannon Fagan

Photo District News, PDN 30 2001

A moment's insight is sometimes worth
a life's experience.
Oliver Wendell Holmes, American scientist,
essayist, poet

A veces, un momento de percepción interior
vale tanto como la experiencia de una vida.
Oliver Wendell Holmes, científico,
ensayista y poeta estadounidense

La vision d'un moment vaut parfois
l'expérience de toute une vie.
Oliver Wendell Holmes, scientifique,
essayiste et poète américain

Die Erkenntnis eines Moments ist
manchmal die Erfahrung eines ganzen
Lebens wert.
Oliver Wendell Holmes, amerikanischer
Wissenschaftler, Essayschreiber und Dichter

Jens Lucking

Association of Photographers 2002

How extraordinary ordinary things are,
like the nature of the mind and the process
of observing.
Norman MacCaig, Scottish poet

Qué extraordinarias son las cosas
ordinarias, como la naturaleza de la mente
y el proceso de la observación.
Norman MacCaig, poeta escocés

Combien extraordinaires sont les choses
ordinaires, comme la nature de l'esprit et
le processus d'observation.
Norman MacCaig, poète écossais

Wie außergewöhnlich gewöhnliche Dinge
doch sind, wie die Natur des Geistes und
der Vorgang des Betrachtens.
Norman MacCaig, schottischer Dichter

West Rock

Communication Arts Photography Annual
2001

Art Director: Sylvia Bors

One of the most wonderful things in nature
is a glance of the eye; it transcends speech;
it is the bodily symbol of identity.
Ralph Waldo Emerson, American philosopher,
poet, essayist

La mirada es una de las maravillas de
la naturaleza; trasciende el lenguaje;
es el símbolo fisico de la identidad.
Ralph Waldo Emerson, filósofo, poeta y
ensayista estadounidense

Le regard est l'une des choses les plus
merveilleuses de la nature ; il transcende
la parole ; il est le symbole physique de
l'identité.
Ralph Waldo Emerson, philosophe, poète
et essayiste américain

Eines der schönsten Dinge der Natur ist
der Blick; er ist der Sprache überlegen;
er verkörpert Identität.
Ralph Waldo Emerson, amerikanischer
Philosoph, Dichter, Essayschreiber

Clarissa Leahy

Merit
Association of Photographers 2002

Not only is your story worth telling, but it
can be told in words so painstakingly
eloquent that it becomes a song.
Gloria Naylor, American novelist and educator

Tu historia no sólo merece ser contada,
sino que puede ser contada con palabras
tan cuidadas y elocuentes que se convertirá
en canción.
Gloria Naylor, novelista y educadora
estadounidense

Non seulement votre histoire vaut la peine
d'être racontée, mais elle peut l'être avec
des mots tellement éloquents qu'elle en
devient une chanson.
Gloria Naylor, éducatrice et romancière
américaine

Ihre Geschichte verdient es nicht nur erzählt
zu werden, sie kann in Worten erzählt werden,
die so schmerzhaft eloquent sind, dass
daraus ein Lied wird.
Gloria Naylor, amerikanische Schriftstellerin
und Pädagogin

Association of Photographers 2003

In art economy is always beauty.
Henry James, American-born British writer
and critic

En el arte, la economía es siempre belleza.
Henry James, escritor y crítico británico
nacido en EE.UU.

En art, économie rime avec beauté.
Henry James, écrivain et critique britannique

In der Kunst bedeutet Reduktion
immer Schönheit.
Henry James, in den USA geborener
britischer Schriftsteller und Kritiker

JFB

Photo District News Photo Annual 2002

The true mystery of the world is the visible,
not the invisible.
Oscar Wilde, Anglo-Irish playwright
and novelist

El verdadero misterio del mundo es lo visible,
no lo invisible.
Oscar Wilde, dramaturgo y novelista
angloirlandés

Le vrai mystère du monde est le visible,
non l'invisible.
Oscar Wilde, romancier et auteur dramatique
anglo-irlandais

Das wahre Mysterium dieser Welt liegt im
Sichtbaren, nicht im Unsichtbaren.
Oscar Wilde, anglo-irischer Dramatiker
und Schriftsteller

Merit
Association of Photographers 2002

A picture is a poem without words.
Confucius, Chinese philosopher

Un cuadro es un poema sin palabras.
Confucius, filósofo chino

Une image est un poème sans les mots.
Confucius, philosophe chinois

Ein Bild ist ein Gedicht ohne Worte.
Confucius, chinesischer Philosoph

Terry Vine

Photo District News Self Promotion
Awards 2002

A photograph is always invisible,
it is not it that we see.
Roland Barthes, French historian,
writer, philosopher

Una fotografía siempre es invisible;
no es ella lo que vemos.
Roland Barthes, historiador, escritor y
filósofo francés

Une photographie est toujours invisible,
ce n'est pas elle que l'on voit.
Roland Barthes, historien, philosophe
et écrivain français

Eine Fotografie ist stets unsichtbar –
sie ist nicht das, was wir sehen.
Roland Barthes, französischer Historiker,
Schriftsteller, Philosoph

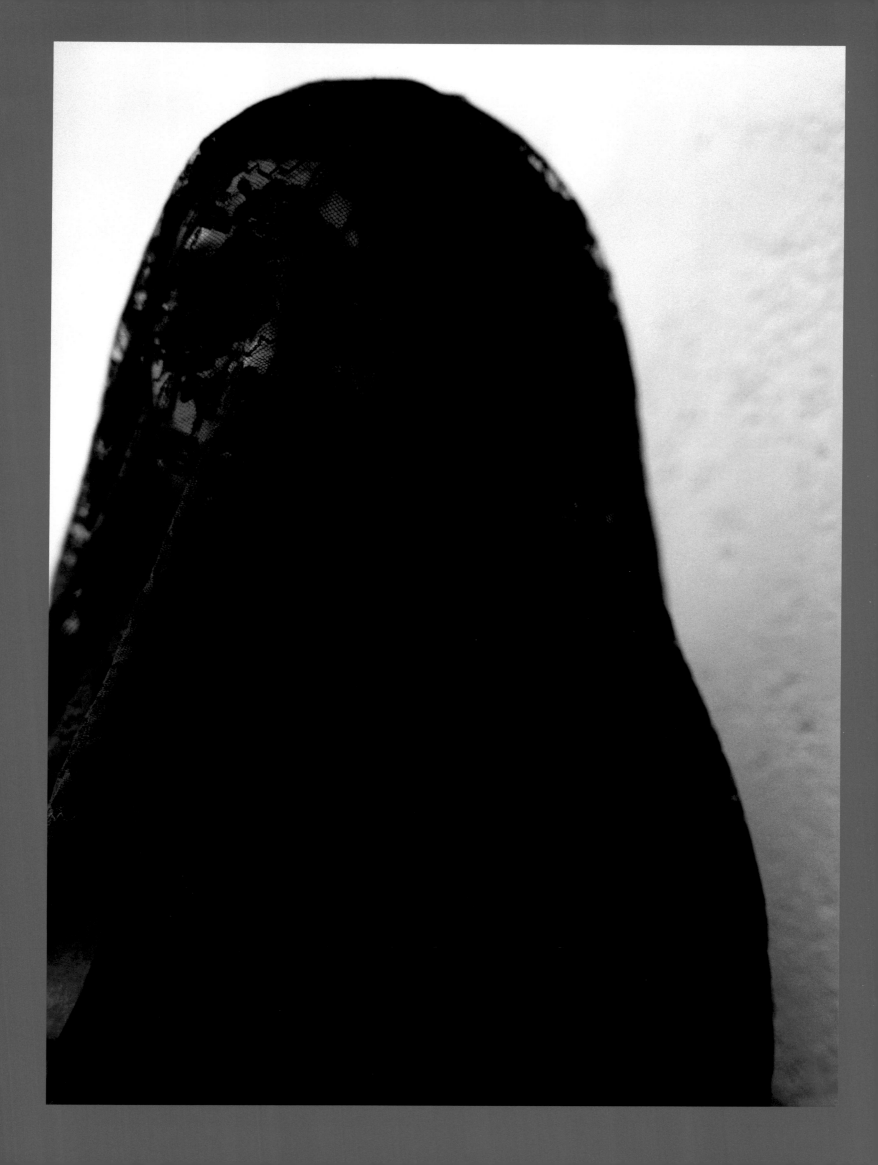

Catherine Ledner

American Photography 18

Art Director: Jennifer Dorn

Character is the interpretation of habits.
John Dewey, American philosopher and
educator

El carácter es la interpretación de
los hábitos.
John Dewey, filósofo y educador
estadounidense

Le caractère est l'interprétation
des habitudes.
John Dewey, philosophe et éducateur
américain

Charakter ist die Interpretation von
Gewohnheiten.
John Dewey, amerikanischer Philosoph
und Pädagoge

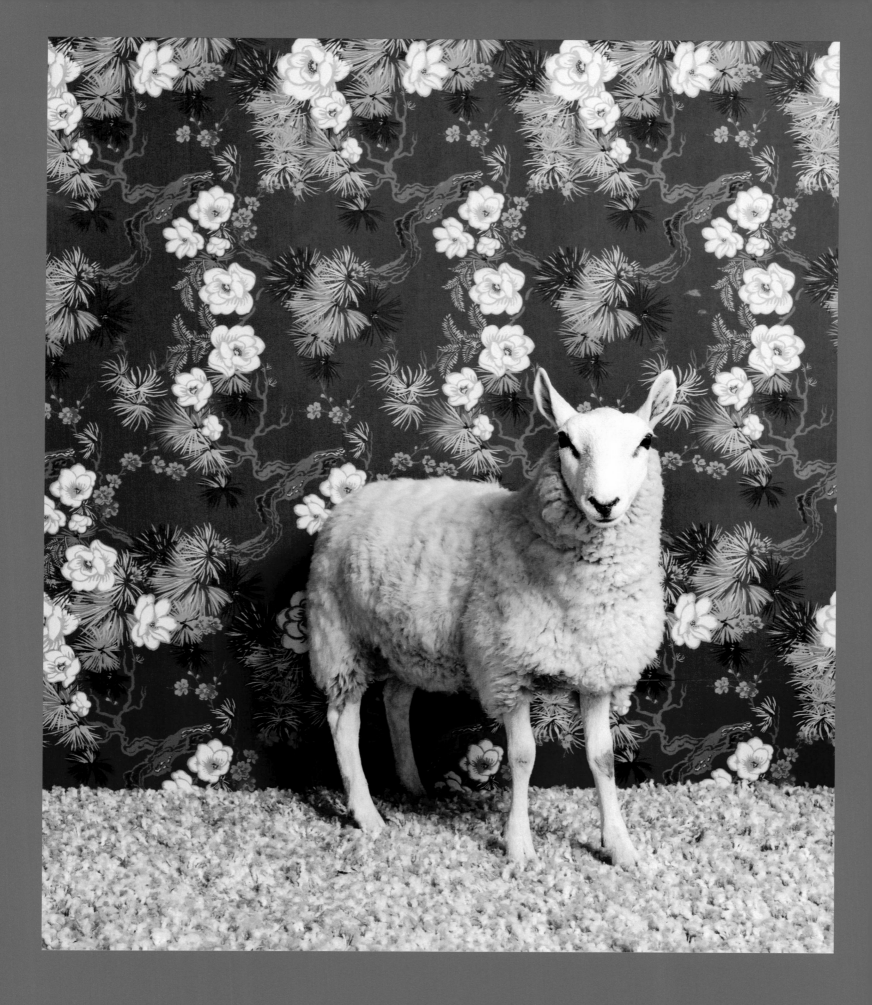

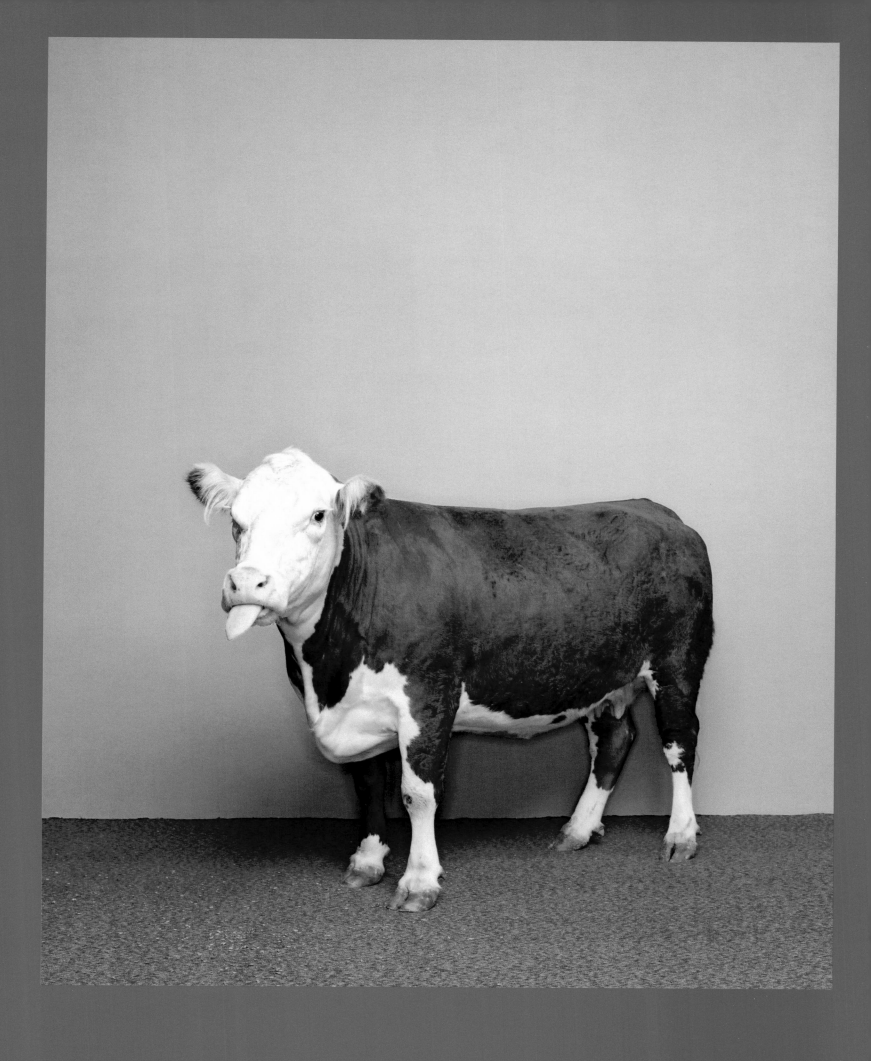

Communication Arts Photography Annual
2001

A photograph can be an instant of life
captured for eternity that will never cease
looking back at you.
Brigitte Bardot, French actress

Una fotografía puede ser un instante de
la vida capturado para la eternidad, que
nunca cesará de devolverte la mirada.
Brigitte Bardot, actriz francesa

Une photographie peut être un instant de
vie capturé pour l'éternité qui ne cessera
jamais de vous regarder.
Brigitte Bardot, actrice française

Eine Fotografie kann ein Moment des
Lebens sein,für die Ewigkeit festgehalten,
der dich nie mehr loslässt.
Brigitte Bardot, französische Schauspielerin

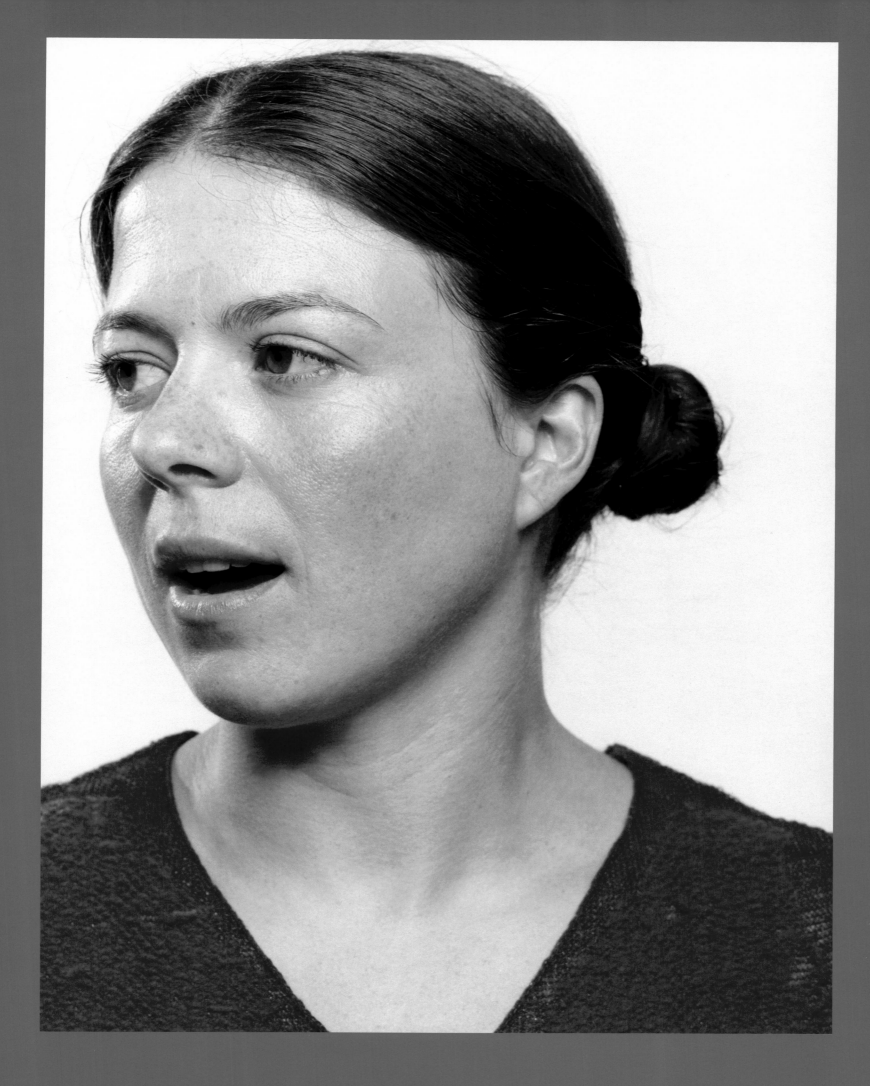

Chip Forelli

Photo District News Photo Annual 2002

All that we see or seem, is but a dream
within a dream.
Edgar Allan Poe, American poet and writer

Todo lo que vemos o parecemos es sólo
un sueño dentro de otro sueño.
Edgar Allan Poe, poeta y escritor
estadounidense

Tout ce que nous voyons ou croyons n'est
qu'un rêve dans un rêve.
Edgar Allan Poe, écrivain et poète américain

Alles, was wir sehen oder zu sein scheinen,
ist nur ein Traum in einem Traum.
Edgar Allan Poe, amerikanischer Dichter
und Schriftsteller

Make visible what, without you,
might perhaps never have been seen.
Robert Bresson, French film director

Fotografía de actualidad y deportiva

Haz visible aquello que, sin ti, quizá
no hubiera sido visto jamás.
Robert Bresson, director de cine francés

Rendre visible ce que l'on n'aurait
peut-être, sans vous, jamais vu.
Robert Bresson, réalisateur français

Sport- und Nachrichtenfotografie

Mache sichtbar, was ohne dich
vielleicht niemand gesehen hätte.
Robert Bresson, französischer
Filmregisseur

Ami Vitale

Magazine Photographer of the Year
National Press Photographers Association
2003

Scenes documenting Kashmir's struggle
for freedom, taken in 2002.

Escenas de la lucha por la libertad en
Cachemira, tomadas en 2002.

Scènes illustrant le combat du Cachemire
pour la liberté, photographiées en 2002.

Bilder, die den Unabhängigkeitskampf in
Kashmir dokumentieren. (2002)

Indian Border Security Force soldiers patrol
Dal Lake at Srinagar, Kashmir, India,
in February 2002.

Soldados de las fuerzas de seguridad de la
frontera india patrullan el lago Dal en Srinagar,
Cachemira, India, en febrero de 2002.

Des soldats de la Force de Sécurité à la
frontière indienne patrouillent autour du lac
Dal à Srinagar, Cachemire, Inde. Février 2002.

Indische Grenzsoldaten patrouillieren in Dal
Lake in Srinagar, Provinz Kashmir, Indien.
(Februar 2002)

Award of excellence, Pictures of the Year
International 2003, Magazine Division,
Spot News category (Picture opposite)
(sólo foto en página opuesta)
(photo ci-contre seulement)
(Nur Bild gegenüber)

3rd place, World Press Photo Awards 2003,
General News Stories

3rd place, National Press Photographers
Association 2003, International News Story

Hindu-Muslim riots in the Indian state of
Gujarat, March 2002, precipitated by the
burning of Hindu nationalists in a train car
by Muslims.

Enfrentamientos entre hindúes y musulmanes
en el estado de Gujarat, India, a raíz del incendio
provocado por un ataque musulmán a un tren
cargado de nacionalistas hindúes en 2002.

Emeutes opposant hindous et musulmans
dans l'Etat indien de Gujarat, exacerbées par
l'attentat de musulmans contre des
nationalistes hindous, embrasés dans un
train. 2002.

Gewalttätige Auseinandersetzungen
zwischen Hindus und Muslimen in der
indischen Provinz Gujarat, ausgelöst durch
die Verbrennung hinduistischer Nationalisten
in einem Eisenbahnwagen durch Muslime.
(2002)

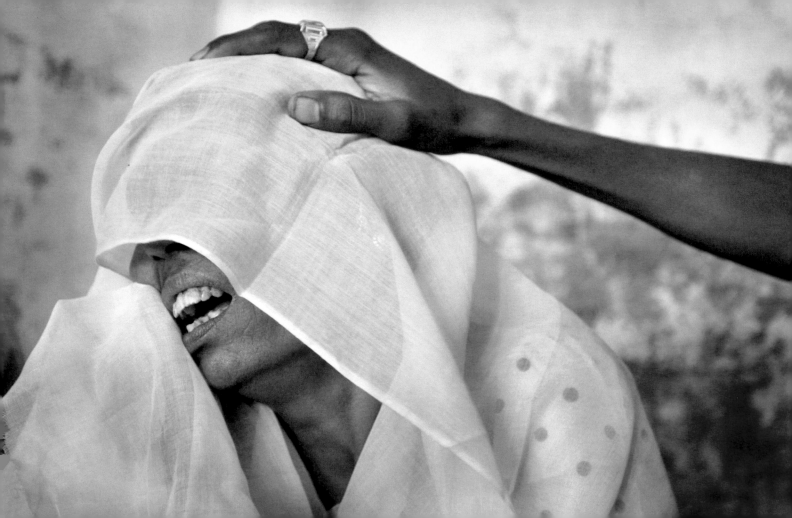

Brent Stirton

2nd place, World Press Photo 2003
Portrait Story

Male members of South Africa's Xhosa tribe during the traditional Circumcision Ceremony. In December 2002, Stirton gained special permission from the Xhosa king to attend this normally secret ceremony.

Varones de la tribu Xhosa de Suráfrica durante la ceremonia tradicional de la circuncisión. En diciembre de 2002, Stirton obtuvo la autorización especial del rey Xhosa para asistir a esta ceremonia, normalmente celebrada en secreto.

Membres de la tribu Xhosa en Afrique du Sud pendant la cérémonie traditionnelle de circoncision. Stirton a obtenu l'autorisation spéciale du roi des Xhosa d'assister à cette cérémonie, habituellement secrète. Décembre 2002.

Männer des südafrikanischen Stammes der Xhosa bei der traditionellen Beschneidungszeremonie. Dank einer Sondererlaubnis des Königs der Xhosa durfte Stirton dieser eigentlich geheimen Zeremonie im Dezember 2002 beiwohnen.

Per-Anders Pettersson

In 2002, Pettersson documented the increase
of child rape in South Africa, a country that
already suffers the highest statistics of rape in
the world.

En 2002, Pettersson documentó el aumento
de las violaciones infantiles en Suráfrica, un
país que ya padece de los más altos índices
de violaciones en el mundo.

En 2002, Pettersson a régulièrement illustré
l'augmentation du nombre de viols d'enfants
en Afrique du Sud, un pays qui affiche déjà les
statistiques les plus élevées au monde en
matière de viols.

2002 dokumentierte Pettersson den Anstieg
von Kindervergewaltigungen in Südafrika,
einem Land, das statistisch ohnehin schon
die meisten Vergewaltigungen weltweit
verzeichnet.

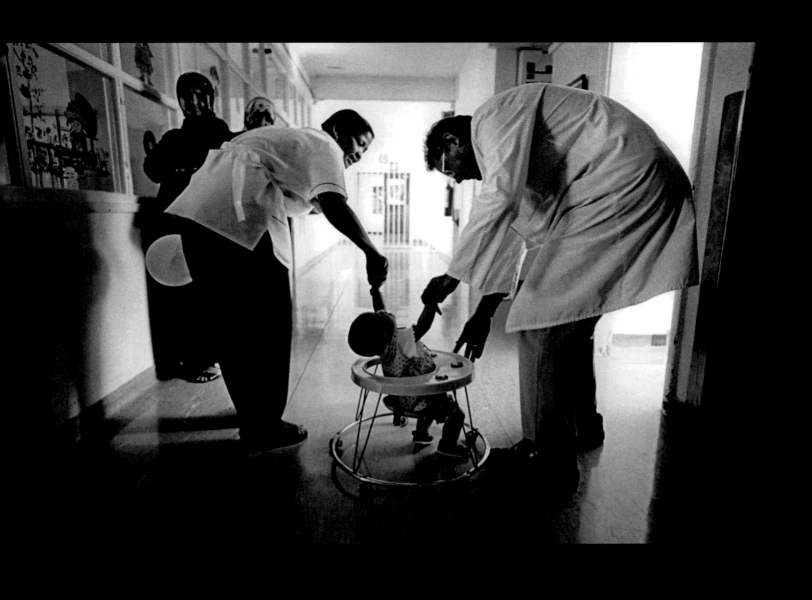

Aleksei Shynkarenko

Honorable Mention, National Press
Photographers Association 2003,
Magazine News

3rd Place, Pictures of the Year International
2003, Newspaper Division, Spot News

An SU-27 fighter jet caught at the point of
impact as it crashes into spectators at an
air show in Lviv, Ukraine, July 2002.

Un caza SU-27, captado por la fotografía
en el momento de estrellarse contra los
espectadores de una exhibición aérea en
Lviv, Ucrania, en julio de 2002.

Un avion de combat SU-27 photographié au
point d'impact alors qu'il s'écrase sur les
spectateurs au cours d'un salon aérien à Lviv
en Ukraine. Juillet 2002.

Ein SU-27 Kampfjet, der bei einer Flugshow
in Lviv in der Ukraine in die Zuschauermenge
stürzt. (Juli 2002)

Scott Nelson

2nd Place, National Press Photographers
Association 2003, Magazine News category

A man and his son watch as U.S. soldiers
prepare to sweep their home in southeastern
Afghanistan, November 2002.

Un hombre y su hijo observan a soldados
estadounidenses que se preparan para barrer
su casa en el sureste de Afganistán, en
noviembre de 2002.

Un homme et son fils regardent les soldats
américains qui s'apprêtent à pulvériser leur
maison dans le sud-est de l'Afghanistan.
Novembre 2002.

Ein Mann und sein Sohn sehen US-Soldaten
dabei zu, wie diese ihr Haus im südöstlichen
Afghanistan durchsuchen. (November 2002)

A Palestinian refugee camp in the West Bank
city of Jenin after an Israeli siege, April 2002.

Un campo de refugiados palestinos en la
ciudad de Jenin, en la Franja Occidental, en
abril de 2002, después de sufrir un sitio israelí.

Un camp de réfugiés palestiniens dans la ville
de Jenin en Cisjordanie après un siège
israélien. Avril 2002.

Ein palästinensisches Flüchtlingslager in
Jenin im Westjordanland nach der
Belagerung durch Israelis. (April 2002)

An Afghan boy blows bubbles given to him by
U.S. Army troops, November 2002.

Un niño afgano hace pompas de jabón con el
aro que le han regalado las tropas
estadounidenses, en noviembre de 2002.

Un jeune garçon afghan fait des bulles de
savon avec un jouet donné par les troupes
de l'armée américaine. Novembre 2002.

Ein afghanischer Junge bläst Seifenblasen;
ein US-Soldat hat es ihm beigebracht.
(November 2002)

Oleg Nikishin

A mother and son in Samara, north of
Baghdad, while a diplomatic solution to
U. S.-Iraqi tensions was being sought,
September 2002.

Una mujer y su hijo en Samara, al norte de
Bagdad, en septiembre de 2002, mientras
se buscaba una solución diplomática a las
tensiones entre EE.UU. e Irak.

Une mère et son fils à Samara, au nord de
Bagdad, tandis que l'on recherche une
solution diplomatique aux tensions opposant
les Etats-Unis et l'Irak. Septembre 2002.

Eine Mutter mit ihrem Sohn im nördlich von
Bagdad gelegenen Samara; zu einer Zeit,
als man noch nach einer friedlichen Lösung
des Konflikts zwischen den USA und dem
Irak suchte. (September 2002)

Honorable Mention, National Press
Photographers Association 2003,
Magazine News Feature Story

In Nahawan, south of Baghdad, children
work, live and play among the smoke and
kilns of the area's many brick factories.

En Nahawan, al sur de Bagdad, los niños
trabajan, viven y juegan entre el humo y los
hornos de las numerosas fábricas de ladrillos
de la zona, en 2002.

A Nahawan, au sud de Bagdad, des enfants
travaillent, vivent et jouent dans la fumée et
les fours de nombreuses briqueteries des
alentours. 2002.

Kinder in Nahawan südlich von Bagdad,
die zwischen den rauchenden Öfen der
Ziegeleien arbeiten, leben und spielen. (2002)

Natalie Behring-Chisholm

Honorable Mention, National Press
Photographers Association 2003,
Magazine News

A French soldier walks past villagers on his
way to an ammunition dump in Dasawe Aole,
north of Kabul, Afghanistan, August 2002.

Un soldado francés, camino de un depósito
de munición, pasa junto a unos pobladores
en Dasawe Aole, al norte de Kabul,
Afganistán, en agosto de 2002.

Un soldat français passe devant des
villageois alors qu'il se dirige vers un dépôt de
munitions à Dasawe Aole, au nord de Kaboul,
Afghanistan. Août 2002.

Ein französischer Soldat auf dem Weg zu
einem Munitionsdepot, vorbei an neugierigen
Dorfbewohnern in Dasawe Aole nördlich von
Kabul. (August 2002)

David Silverman

Honorable Mention, National Press
Photographers Association 2003,
Magazine News

House-to-house searches of a refugee
camp in the West Bank town of Tulkarem,
March 2002.

Inspección realizada casa por casa en
un campo de refugiados de la ciudad
de Tulkarem, en la Franja Occidental,
en marzo de 2002.

Fouille de chacune des habitations dans
un camp de réfugiés à Tulkarem en
Cisjordanie. Mars 2002.

Hausdurchsuchungen in einem
Flüchtlingslager in Tulkarem im
Westjordanland. (März 2002)

Roger Lemoyne

3rd place, National Press Photographers
Association 2003, Magazine News
Feature Story

Afghan families go about their daily lives
amid the ruins of Kabul, 2002.

Familias afganas vuelven a su rutina diaria
entre las ruinas de Kabul, en 2002.

La vie quotidienne de familles afghanes
dans les ruines de Kaboul. 2002.

Der Alltag afghanischer Familien inmitten
der Ruinen von Kabul. (2002)

Tajikistani horsemen playing Buzkashi in
Kabul, Afghanistan, 2002. The rider (or team)
who is able to pitch a dead calf or goat across
a goal line first wins.

Jinetes de Tajikistán juegan al *buzkashi* en
Kabul, Afganistán, en 2002. En este deporte
tradicional, el jinete (o el equipo) que consigue
arrastrar una cabra muerta al campo contrario
gana el encuentro.

Des cavaliers du Tadjikistan jouent au
buzkashi à Kaboul en Afghanistan, 2002.
Le cavalier (ou l'équipe) qui arrive à franchir
en premier la ligne avec une tête de chèvre
ou de veau mort remporte la victoire.

Tadschikische Reiter spielen Buzkashi in
Kabul. Der Reiter (bzw. das Team), der es
schafft, ein totes Kalb oder eine tote Ziege
über die Torlinie zu werfen, hat gewonnen.
(2002)

Clive Mason

Sports Writers'Association, Sport England
Sports Photographer of the Year 2003

Winner, Sports Writers'Association, Sport
England Specialist Portfolio Award 2003

Action taken during the Monaco Formula One
Grand Prix held in Monte Carlo, Monaco,
2002.

Acción candente en la competición por el
Gran Premio de Fórmula Uno de Montecarlo,
Mónaco, 2002.

Action prise pendant le Grand Prix de
Formule 1 à Monte-Carlo. Monaco, 2002.

Während des Formel 1 Grand Prix in Monte
Carlo gemachte Aufnahmen. (Monaco, 2002)

Mike Hewitt

Lleyton Hewitt in action at Wimbledon,
England, June 2002.
Following pages:
Manchester United versus Southampton,
England, January 2002; dog racing in Hove,
England, April 2002.

Lleyton Hewitt en acción en Wimbledon,
Inglaterra, en junio de 2002.
En las páginas siguientes:
Partido Manchester United-Southampton,
Inglaterra, enero de 2002; carreras de perros,
Hove, Inglaterra, abril de 2002.

Lleyton Hewitt en pleine action à Wimbledon,
Angleterre. Juin 2002.
Pages suivantes:
Manchester United contre Southampton,
Angleterre. Janvier 2002 ; courses de chiens à
Hove, Angleterre. Avril 2002.

Lleyton Hewitt in Aktion in Wimbledon.
(Juni 2002)
Folgende Seiten: Manchester United gegen
Southampton. (Januar 2002)
Hunderennen in Hove an der Südküste von
England. (April 2002)

Nick Laham

Thomas Rupprath at the Telstra World Cup
Swimming, Australia, December 2002.
Following pages:
greyhound racing, Australia, April 2002; Anton
King during the Australian Canoe
Championship, March 2002.

Thomas Rupprath en la Copa del Mundo de
Natación de Telstra, Australia, en diciembre
de 2002.
En las páginas siguientes:
carreras de galgos en Australia, abril de 2002;
Anton King durante el Campeonato de
Piragüismo de Australia, en marzo de 2002.

Thomas Rupprath lors de la Coupe du Monde
de Natation parrainée par Telstra, Australie.
Décembre 2002.
Pages suivantes :
Courses de lévriers, Australie. Avril 2002 ;
Anton King durant le Championnat australien
de canoë. Mars 2002.

Thomas Rupprath bei der Telstra
Schwimmweltmeisterschaft in Australien.
(Dezember 2002)
Folgende Seiten:
Windhundrennen in Australien. (April 2002)
Anton King bei der australischen
Kanumeisterschaft. (März 2002)

Laurence Griffiths

England soccer coach Sven Goran-Eriksson
during training, November 2001.

Sven-Goran Eriksson, técnico del
seleccionado inglés de fútbol, durante un
entrenamiento en noviembre de 2001.

Sven Goran-Eriksson, entraîneur de l'équipe
de football d'Angleterre, à l'œuvre.
Novembre 2001.

Der englische Nationaltrainer Sven-Göran
Eriksson beim Training. (November 2001)

Donald Miralle

Sasakawa World Sports Federation Contest
2002, Special Photographers Award, Portfolio

Jeff Hubbard surfs in front of the Queen Mary
cruise liner at Long Beach, California,
June 2000.
Following pages:
Lenny Krayzelburg wins the 100m backstroke
at the Janet Evans International Meet,
Los Angeles, California, July 2000; Cory
McFadden during the Pro Bull Riders
Bud Light Cup in Anaheim, California,
February 2001.

El surfista Jeff Hubbard pasa frente al
transatlántico Queen Mary en Long Beach,
California, en junio de 2000.
En las páginas siguientes:
Lenny Krayzelburg gana los 100 m espalda
en el Encuentro Internacional Janet Evans de
Los Ángeles, California, en julio de 2000; Cory
McFadden durante la competición Pro Bull
Riders Bud Light Cup en Anaheim, California,
en febrero de 2001.

Jeff Hubbard surfe devant le paquebot
"Queen Mary" à Long Beach, Californie.
Juin 2000.
Pages suivantes :
Lenny Krayzelburg remporte le 100 m en dos
crawlé au Janet Evans International Meet à
Los Angeles, Californie. Juillet 2000 ; Cory
McFadden pendant la Pro Bull Riders Bud
Light Cup à Anaheim, Californie. Février 2001.

Surfer Jeff Hubbard vor dem Kreuzfahrtschiff
Queen Mary vor Long Beach, Kalifornien.
(Juni 2000)
Folgende Seiten:
Lenny Krayzelburg gewinnt die 100 m Rücken
beim Janet Evans International Meet in Los
Angeles. (Juli 2000)
Cory McFadden beim Pro Bull Riders Bud
Light Cup in Anaheim, Kalifornien.
(Februar 2001)

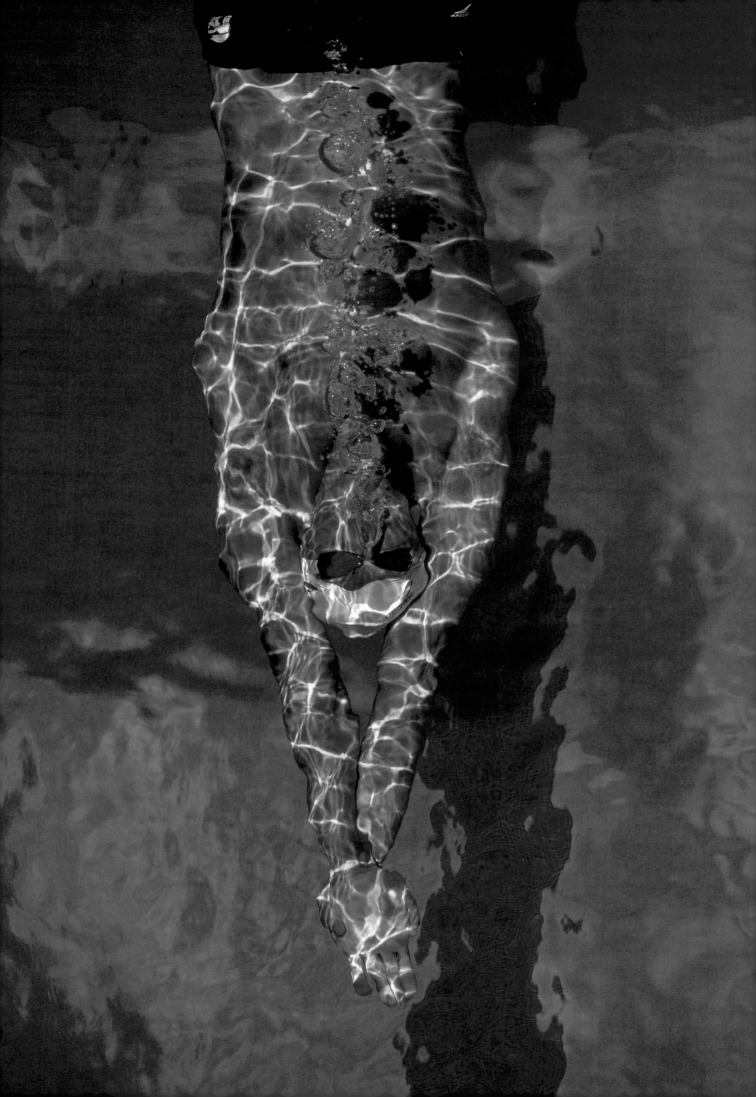

Hong Kong's Mark Kin Ming Kwok during the
2002 Pan Pacific Swimming Championships.

Mark Kin Ming Kwok, de Hong-Kong, durante
el Campeonato de Natación Pan Pacific 2002
en Yokohama, Japón.

Mark Kin Ming Kwok de Hongkong durant le
Championnat Pan Pacific de Natation 2002 à
Yokohama, Japon.

Mark Kin Ming Kwok aus Hong Kong bei den
Pan Pacific Schwimmmeisterschaften in
Yokohama, Japan. (2002)

タウンスポーツ

Oakland Raider Jerry Porter, yelling during a game against the San Diego Chargers, California, November 2001.

Jerry Porter, de los Oakland Raiders, grita durante un juego contra los San Diego Chargers en California, en noviembre de 2001.

Jerry Porter des Oakland Raiders, hurlant pendant un match contre les San Diego Chargers, Californie. Novembre 2001.

Footballspieler Jerry Porter von den Oakland Raiders in Aktion beim Spiel gegen die San Diego Chargers in Kalifornien. (November 2001)

Ezra Shaw

Scenes from the 2002 Tour de France,
taken from Shaw's picture story of
Lance Armstrong.

Escenas del Tour de France 2002, tomadas
del reportaje fotográfico sobre Lance Shaw
realizado por Shaw.

Scènes du Tour de France 2002, extraites du
livre-album de Shaw sur Lance Armstrong.

Szenen von der Tour de France 2002 aus
Shaws Bilderstrecke über Lance Armstrong.

New England Patriot Bobby Hamilton
celebrates victory in the snow after his team's
near defeat during the AFC playoffs, Foxboro,
Massachusetts, January 2002.

Bobby Hamilton, de los New England
Patriots, celebra la victoria en la nieve,
después de su equipo estuviera a punto de
ser derrotado en los *playoffs* de la AFC en
Foxboro, Massachussetts, en enero de 2002.

Bobby Hamilton des New England Patriots
célèbre la victoire dans la neige après que son
équipe a frôlé la défaite lors des séries
éliminatoires de l'AFC à Foxboro,
Massachusetts. Janvier 2002.

Footballspieler Bobby Hamilton von den New
England Patriots feiert den knappen Sieg
seines Teams im Schneetreiben bei den AFC
Playoffs im Foxboro Stadion von
Massachusetts. (Januar 2002)

Bibliography
Bibliografía
Bibliographie
Literaturnachweis

Bacon, Sir Francis (1561-1626)
'Of Beauty,' *Essays*, 1998.
Bardot, Brigitte (b.1934)
The Book of Quotes, Barbara Rowes, 1979.
Barthes, Roland (1915-1980)
Camera Lucida: Reflections on Photography,
1982.
Bresson, Robert (1907-1999)
'1950-1958: The Real,' *Notes on the
Cinematographer*, 1975.
Confucius (551-479 B.C.)
Dewey, John (1859-1952)
Human Nature and Conduct, 1922.
Emerson, Ralph Waldo (1803-1882)
Correct Quotes for DOS, WordStar
International, 1991.
Harris, Lauren (1819-1880)
Holmes, Oliver Wendell (1809-1894)
The Professor at the Breakfast-Table, 1872.
James, Henry (1843-1916)
'Prefaces,' *The Altar of the Dead*, 1909.
James, William (1842-1910)
*Essays in Radical Empiricism & A Pluralistic
Universe*, 1967.
Kazantzakis, Nikos (1883-1957)
Zorba the Greek, 1996.
MacCaig, Norman (1910-1996)
'An Ordinary Day,' *Surroundings*, 1966.

Meredith, George (1828-1909)
'The Woods of Westermain,' *Poems Volume
II*, 1910.
Michaels, Anne (b.1958)
'Lake of Two Rivers,' *The Weight of Oranges*,
1997.
Naylor, Gloria (b.1950)
African American Writers, Valerie Smith, 2000.
Picasso, Pablo (1881-1973)
Success and Failure of Picasso, John Berger,
1965.
Poe, Edgar Allan (1809-1849)
'A Dream within a Dream,' *The Complete
Tales and Poems of Edgar Allan Poe*, 1987.
Rodin, Auguste (1840-1917)
Rodin, Bernard Champigneulle, J. Maxwell
Brownjohn, 1967.
Sontag, Susan (b.1933)
New York Review of Books, April 18, 1974.
Wilde, Oscar (1854-1900)
*Pearls of Wisdom: A Harvest of Quotations
from All Ages*, Jerome Agel, Walter Glanze,
1987.
Wittgenstein, Ludwig (1889-1951)
Remarks on Colour, 1978.

For further information about Getty Images and our range of products and services, please contact us.

Si deseas más información acerca de Getty Images y de nuestra gama de productos y servicios, contacta con nosotros.

Pour en savoir plus sur Getty Images et notre gamme de produits et services, veuillez nous contacter.

Für weitere Informationen über Getty Images, unsere Produkte oder unsere Services wenden Sie sich bitte an uns.

Africa
Gallo Images
Telephone: +27 11 783 3800
Email: sales@galloimages.co.za

gettyimages.com

Argentina
Luis Rosendo Producciones Fotográficas
Telephone: +54 (11) 4374 3330
Email: info@luisrosendo.com.ar

gettyimages.com

Australia
Getty Images
Telephone: 1800 500 141
Email: info.asiapac@gettyimages.com

gettyimages.com

Austria
Getty Images
Telephone: 0800 999 611
Email: sales.austria@getty-images.com

gettyimages.de

Baltics
Getty Images
Telephone: +44 20 7544 3400
Email: info.baltics@gettyimages.com

gettyimages.com

Belgium
Getty Images
Telephone: 0800 48 285
Email: info.belgium@getty-images.com

gettyimages.com

Brazil
Getty Images
Telephone: 0800 772 2074
Email: info@gettyimages.com.br

gettyimages.com

Central Europe
Getty Images
Telephone: +44 20 7544 3400
Email: centraleuropeansales@gettyimages.com

gettyimages.com

Chile
The Image Bank Chile
Telephone: +56 2 737 8880
Email: tibchile@theimagebank.co.cl

gettyimages.com

Colombia
Photos Images Ltda.
Telephone: +57 (1) 635 7576
Email: photoima@cable.net.co

gettyimages.com

Costa Rica
Fotos IMAGEN SA
Telephone: +506 221 5852
Email: fotoscr@racsa.co.cr

gettyimages.com

Denmark
Getty Images
Telephone: 80 88 43 19
Email: kundeservice@gettyimages.com

gettyimages.com

Ecuador
Photos Images Cia. Ltda.
Telephone: +593 2 244 5573
Email: phimages@hoy.net

gettyimages.com

Finland
Getty Images
Telephone: 0800 118 988
Email: asiakaspalvelu@getty-images.com

gettyimages.com

France
Getty Images
Telephone: 08 05 11 14 13
appel gratuit depuis la France
Telephone: 08 00 00 01 80
appel gratuit depuis la Suisse
Email: info.paris@getty-images.com

gettyimages.fr

Germany
Getty Images
Creative Telephone: 0800 101 3135
Creative Email: sales.germany@getty-images.com
News & Sport Telephone: 0800 101 4062

gettyimages.de

Greece
Ideal Image
Telephone: +30 210 61 97 506
Email: info-stills@idealimagegreece.com

gettyimages.com

Holland
Getty Images
Telephone: 0800 023 4532
Email: info.holland@getty-images.com

gettyimages.com

Hong Kong
Getty Images
Telephone: +852 2574 7788
Email: info.asiapac@gettyimages.com

gettyimages.com

Hungary
ASM Europress
Telephone: +36 1 356 5451
Email: foto@europress.hu

gettyimages.com

Iceland
Nordic Photos
Telephone: +35 4562 5900
Email: kjartan@nordicphotos.com

gettyimages.com

Ireland
Getty Images
Telephone: 1800 931 768
Email: sales@gettyimages.co.uk

gettyimages.co.uk

Israel
Mar'ot Images
Telephone: +972 3 510 4382
Email: sales@imagebank.org.il

gettyimages.com

Italy
Laura Ronchi
Telephone: +39 02 481 9020
Email: info@lauraronchi.com

gettyimages.com

Japan
Getty Images
Creative Telephone: 0120-369-299
Creative Email: info.japan@gettyimages.com
News & Sport Telephone: 03-3546-2700
News & Sport Email: press@aflo.com

gettyimages.com

Luxembourg
Getty Images
Telephone: +31 20 502 5329
Email: info.belgium@getty-images.com

gettyimages.com

Malaysia
Getty Images
Telephone: +60 3 2710 3448
Email: info.asiapac@gettyimages.com

gettyimages.com

Mexico
R.V.G. Bartolomé S.A. de C.V.
Telephone: +52 (55) 5660 2909
Email: novel@imagebank.com.mx

gettyimages.com

New Zealand
Getty Images
Telephone: 0800 462 431
Email: info.asiapac@gettyimages.com

gettyimages.com

Norway
Getty Images
Telephone: 800 16 391
Email: info.norway@gettyimages.com

gettyimages.com

Paraguay
Paraguay Imágenes S.R.L.
Telephone: 595 21 295 413
Email: asuncine@asuncine.com

gettyimages.com

Peru
Kawas y Salinas S.A.C.
Telephone: +51 (1) 444 3330
Email: imagebank@terra.com.pe

gettyimages.com

Philippines
Getty Images
Telephone: +63 2 810 9026
Email: info.asiapac@gettyimages.com

gettyimages.com

Poland
Flash Press Media
Telephone: +48 22 843 90 92
Email: info@fpm.com.pl

gettyimages.com

Portugal
Image One
Telephone: +351 21 458 7430
Email: imageone@imageone.pt

gettyimages.com

Romania
Guliver
Telephone: +40 21 310 2663
Email: office@guliver.ro

gettyimages.com

Russia
Fotobank
Telephone: +7 095 787 7003
Email: fotobank@fotobank.com

gettyimages.com

Singapore
Getty Images
Telephone: +65 6227 6118
Email: info.asiapac@gettyimages.com

gettyimages.com

Spain
Getty Images
Telephone: 800 099 250
Email: info.spain@gettyimages.es

gettyimages.es

Sweden
Getty Images
Telephone: 0200 88 75 14
Email: info.sweden@gettyimages.com

gettyimages.com

Switzerland
Getty Images
Telephone: 0800 000 180
Email: sales.switzerland@gettyimages.com

gettyimages.de

Thailand
Getty Images
Telephone: +66 2 266 4233
Email: info.asiapac@gettyimages.com

gettyimages.com

Turkey
Serimaj
Telephone: +90 212 272 4232
Email: info@serimaj.com

gettyimages.com

United Arab Emirates
CDI the image library
Telephone: +971 4 286 8622
Email: sales@cdi.co.ae

gettyimages.com

United Kingdom
Getty Images
Creative Telephone: 0800 376 7977
Creative Email: sales@gettyimages.co.uk
News & Sport Telephone: 0800 376 7981
News & Sport Email:
europeannewsandsport@gettyimages.com

gettyimages.co.uk

United States of America & Canada
Getty Images
Creative Telephone: 800 IMAGERY (462 4379)
Creative Email: sales@gettyimages.com
News & Sport Telephone: +1 646 613 3676
News & Sport Email:
northamericannewsandsport@gettyimages.com

gettyimages.com

Uruguay
Londinux S.A.
Telephone: +598 2 418 1689
Email: imagebank@londinux.com.uy

gettyimages.com